COFFEE
GIVES ME SUPERPOWERS

AN ILLUSTRATED BOOK ABOUT THE MOST AWESOME BEVERAGE ON EARTH

RYOKO IWATA

I ♥ COFFEE.JP

Andrews McMeel Publishing®

Kansas City · Sydney · London

SIP IT SLOWLY.
THIS BOOK IS HIGHLY CAFFEINATED.

CONTENTS

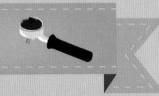

SHOULD YOU PUT COFFEE

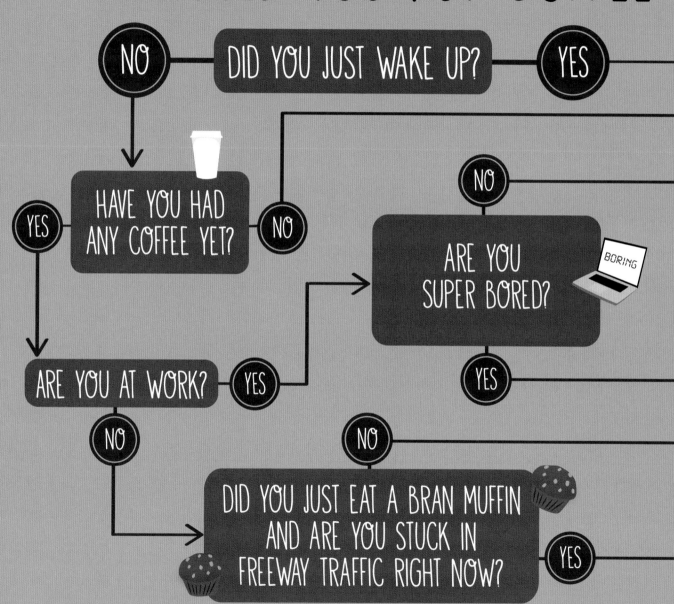

DID YOU JUST WAKE UP?

NO

YES

HAVE YOU HAD ANY COFFEE YET?

YES

NO

ARE YOU SUPER BORED?

BORING

NO

YES

ARE YOU AT WORK?

YES

NO

NO

DID YOU JUST EAT A BRAN MUFFIN AND ARE YOU STUCK IN FREEWAY TRAFFIC RIGHT NOW?

YES

IN YOUR FACE RIGHT NOW?

WILL YOU BE BORED LATER?
(AN UPCOMING MEETING, FOR EXAMPLE)

YES

NO

YOU DEFINITELY NEED TO PUT SOME COFFEE IN THAT GOOD-LOOKING FACE OF YOURS.

LIAR.
THE FUTURE IS ALWAYS BORING UNLESS THERE'S COFFEE IN IT.

YOU MIGHT WANT TO HOLD OFF ON THE COFFEE FOR A BIT.

YOUR BRAIN

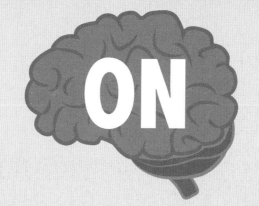

ON

BEER
vs.
COFFEE

HOW YOUR BRAIN WORKS

This part of the brain is called **the cerebral cortex.**
The cerebral cortex controls conscious thought, language, and interaction.

When alcohol hits your cerebral cortex, you feel less focused, but it frees up your brain from all the distractions that normally occupy it.

AND WHEN YOUR BLOOD ALCOHOL REACHES 0.07
(ABOUT 2 DRINKS' WORTH)

YOU BECOME MORE CREATIVE!!

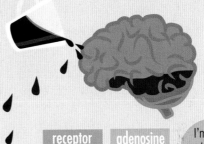

receptor adenosine

I'm the one controlling your energy level.

ZZZZ......

When adenosine binds with its adenosine receptor, you feel DROWSY.

When caffeine comes in, the receptor binds with caffeine instead of adenosine.

caffeine

WHICH MEANS 15 MINUTES LATER,

YOU HAVE MORE ENERGY!!

THE GOOD

Beer makes you less worried about the world around you, which frees up your brain to make deeper connections and **come up with great ideas.**

Caffeine's effects kick in after only 15 minutes, giving you **more energy and a stronger ability to focus.**

THE BAD

Drinking a couple of beers makes you **less focused** and decreases your memory.

Drinking even small amounts of coffee will result in a **tolerance** and your body will need more to get the same stimulation.

THE BEST TIME TO DRINK

Beer is good **if you are searching for an initial idea.**

Coffee is good **if you've already got an idea and you just need to focus on the busywork.**

Although!

DRINK TOO MUCH OF EITHER, AND YOU'LL LOSE THE BENEFITS OF BOTH.
EVERYTHING IN MODERATION, FOLKS.

CONCLUSION

THE IDEA

THE EXECUTION

 Beer is good for kickstarting your brain into coming up with great ideas.

Coffee is good for executing those ideas.

The best time to drink

coffee

according to science!

Your body works on a rhythm

and is guided by what is known as your

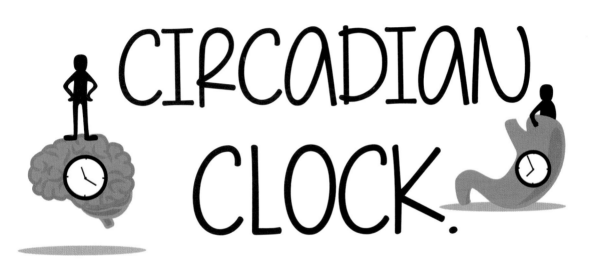

CIRCADIAN CLOCK.

Your circadian clock is a 24-hour hormonal cycle that occurs within your body. It tells you when it's time to wake, eat, sleep, and do a variety of other things.

At a certain point in this rhythm,  **cortisol**

is produced—a hormone that makes you feel awake and alert.

Production of cortisol peaks between 8 a.m. and 9 a.m.,
meaning your body is **naturally caffeinating** itself
(albeit without caffeine) during these hours of the day.

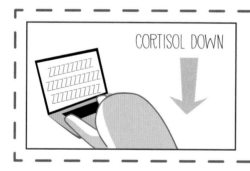

CORTISOL DOWN

CORTISOL UP

I LOVE TYPING!

If you drink coffee at the same time that your cortisol levels
are peaking, the effects of caffeine will be greatly diminished,
since you're already experiencing a natural jolt.

By consuming caffeine when it is not needed, your body will build a tolerance to it faster, and the buzz you get from it will greatly diminish.

So, if you find yourself upping your daily caffeine dosage to get the boost you want, instead try drinking your coffee AFTER your cortisol levels have dropped, which happens a few times a day. The first drop occurs between 9:30 a.m. and 11:30 a.m.

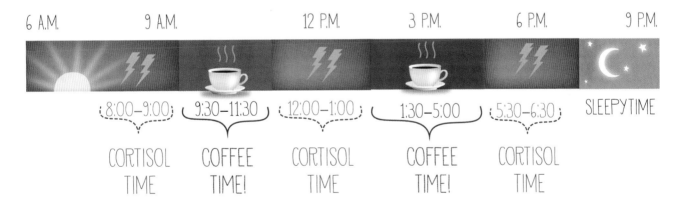

| 6 A.M. | 9 A.M. | 12 P.M. | 3 P.M. | 6 P.M. | 9 P.M. |

8:00-9:00 — CORTISOL TIME

9:30-11:30 — COFFEE TIME!

12:00-1:00 — CORTISOL TIME

1:30-5:00 — COFFEE TIME!

5:30-6:30 — CORTISOL TIME

SLEEPYTIME

The End!

THE

6

WORST TYPES
OF
COFFEE DRINKERS

1. THE HIGH MAINTENANCE

I'll have an extra-hot-no-whip-skinny-half-shot-hazelnut-venti-soy-bungleberry-crappuchino.

I'm gonna need that delivered to my castle in the next five minutes, preferably via pony.

2. THE SNOB

You shouldn't drink coffee that's made by "the corporations," okay? Also, it's pronounced "espresso," not "eXpresso."

Also, real coffee must first be cleansed in the tears of sacred Peruvian yaks.

Also, I have no friends.

3. THE OVER-CAFFEINATED NEWBIE

I HAVE ACHIEVED ENLIGHTENMENT FROM THREE SIPS OF COFFEE!
HOLY-GOSH-DARN-YIPPEE I AM EXCITED!

LET'S DISCUSS BUSINESS WAIT NEVER MIND
LET'S DISCUSS THE WEATHER WAIT NEVER MIND
LET'S VIBRATE IN PLACE AND TAKE TURNS CUTTING
EACH OTHER OFF IN CONVERSATION!!!

WEEEEE HAHAHA YES THAT SOUNDS NICE I AM SO FREAKING BUZZED RIGHT NOW.

4. THE DARK LORD OF BLACK COFFEE

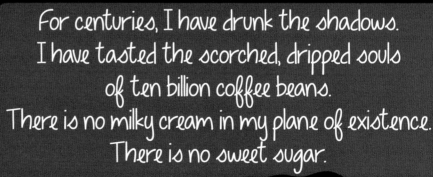

For centuries, I have drunk the shadows.
I have tasted the scorched, dripped souls
of ten billion coffee beans.
There is no milky cream in my plane of existence.
There is no sweet sugar.
There is only DARKNESS.

5. THE DECORATOR

I love coffee!
Actually, I love cream, sugar, syrup, sprinkles, and all the other crap I put in here to cover up the actual taste of coffee.
Seriously, this is so over-sweetened I could be drinking belly button lint mixed with water and I'd never know the difference.

6. THE STRESS JUNKIE

I HAVEN'T SLEPT IN A YEAR AND IF YOU GET BETWEEN ME AND MY COFFEE I WILL MURDER YOU AND FEED YOUR REMAINS TO THE SQUIRRELS THAT NEST BEHIND MY HOUSE.

COFFEE WORLDWIDE

The world consumes
1.6 billion cups
of coffee daily.

Coffee is
the second most
traded product in the world
after petroleum.

One-third of all
coffee in the world comes
from **Brazil.**

The world record for
most coffee consumption is
**82 cups in
7 hours.**

TOP COFFEE-DRINKING COUNTRIES

1 FINLAND

2 NORWAY

3 ICELAND

THE WORLD'S MOST EXPENSIVE COFFEE

Black Ivory Coffee, which comes from elephant poop, is now the most expensive coffee in the world.

2 cups for $50

COFFEE IN THE U.S.

There are about **100 million** coffee drinkers in the U.S.

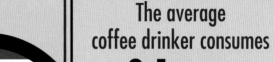

The average coffee drinker consumes **3.1 cups** of coffee daily.

American workers spend about **$20 per week** on coffee.

America spends **$4 billion** importing coffee each year.

1,640 shops

Seattle has the most coffee shops (per capita) in the U.S.

HAWAII

Hawaii is the only U.S. state that grows coffee commercially.

THE TOP THREE MOST CAFFEINATED CITIES

1 SEATTLE, WA

2 PORTLAND, OR

3 SAN JOSE, CA

AMERICA CONSUMES
400 MILLION CUPS OF COFFEE DAILY

That's enough to fill 14.2 Statues of Liberty!

A few bits of trivia worth knowing

COFFEE IS TECHNICALLY MADE OUT OF

FRUIT!

HECK, YES!
That takes care of that food group!

THE BEST TIME FOR A COFFEE IS AROUND 2:00 P.M.

Studies have shown that most people's energy levels are at their lowest at about 2:16 p.m.

COFFEE HAS

0
calories

(Unless you drown it in cream and sugar, of course.)

A GRANDE COFFEE CONTAINS THE CAFFEINE EQUIVALENT OF 9.5 CANS OF COKE

16 oz. =

IT TAKES 40 COFFEE BEANS TO MAKE AN ESPRESSO

AND LAST,
THE LETHAL DOSE OF COFFEE FOR AN ADULT IS 100 CUPS

A map of which U.S. states have the

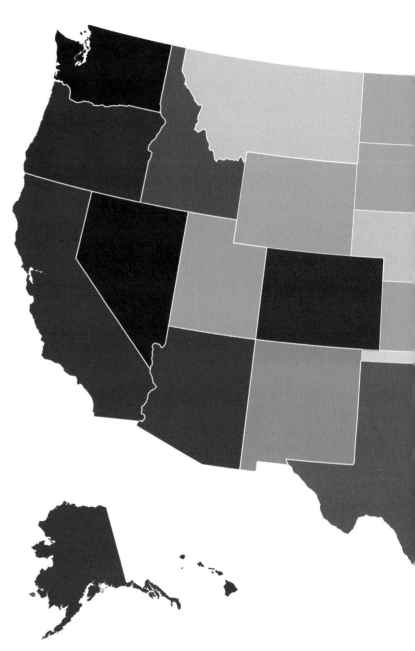

most **STARBUCKS** (per capita)

most — least

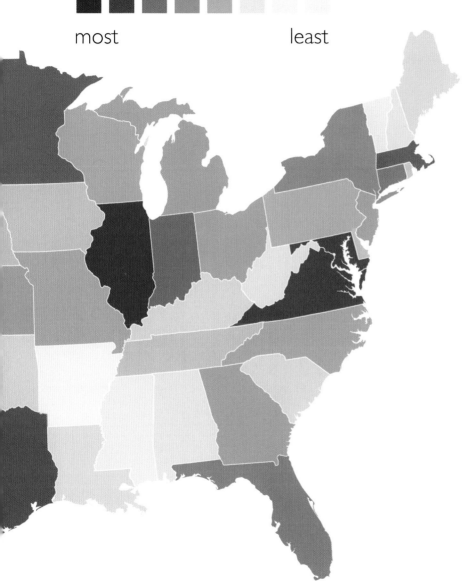

#26 Ohio
#27 South Dakota
#28 New Jersey
#29 Kansas
#30 Michigan
#31 Missouri
#32 North Carolina
#33 Wisconsin
#34 Pennsylvania
#35 Tennessee
#36 Nebraska
#37 Montana
#38 Iowa
#39 Rhode Island
#40 Maine
#41 South Carolina
#42 Kentucky
#43 Oklahoma
#44 Louisiana
#45 Alabama
#46 New Hampshire
#47 West Virginia
#48 Mississippi
#49 Vermont
#50 Arkansas

ESPRESSO DRINKS 101

{ IN ITALIAN, ESPRESSO MEANS "PRESS OUT" AND "FAST,"
AND IT'S CREATED BY A MACHINE THAT PRESSES
HOT, PRESSURIZED WATER THROUGH FINELY GROUND COFFEE. }

THIS IS ESPRESSO.

- A BIG DIFFERENCE FROM DRIP COFFEE IS THAT ESPRESSO HAS "CREMA," WHICH IS A THIN LAYER OF FOAM AT THE TOP.

- ESPRESSO HAS MORE FLAVOR AND LESS BITTERNESS THAN DRIP COFFEE BECAUSE IT'S BREWED QUICKLY WHILE UNDER HIGH AMOUNTS OF PRESSURE.

BASIC ESPRESSO DRINKS

Hot Water

Espresso

AMERICANO

Milk Foam

Steamed Milk

Espresso

CAFÉ LATTE

Milk Foam

Steamed Milk

Espresso

CAPPUCCINO

Whipped Cream

Steamed Milk

Chocolate Syrup

Espresso

CAFÉ MOCHA

Milk Foam

Espresso

MACCHIATO

Double Shot
Espresso

DOPPIO

Half & Half

Espresso

BREVE

Whipped Cream

Espresso

CON PANNA

Sugar

Steamed Milk

Espresso

CAFÉ CON LECHE

HONEYBEES
are
NATURE'S LITTLE COFFEE ADDICTS

As you may know, coffee beans come from coffee trees. Coffee trees produce coffee cherries, which contain seeds. Those seeds are the coffee beans you grind up for your daily fix.

Do you know **why** coffee trees have caffeine?

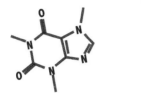

Is it to give us humans *awesome zippy powers?*

Nope!

Caffeine is a coffee tree's defense mechanism.
It has toxic concentrations of caffeine in the leaves,
which are poisonous to garden slugs,
and act as a natural pesticide.

HOWEVER,

we humans love that poison dearly.
We absolutely *love* it.

WHY?

→ It's not poisonous to us.

(Unless you drank a lethal dose, which for a human being is about 100 cups of coffee.)

→ It helps you concentrate.

→ It improves your long-term memory.

→ Coffee is crazy delicious.

And there's one other creature on this planet that enjoys caffeine as much as we do.

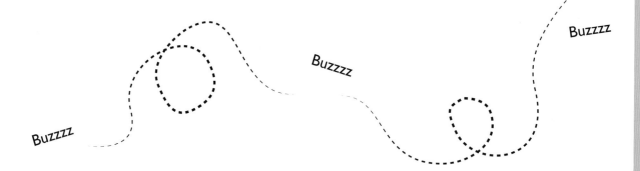

Buzzzz

Buzzzz

Buzzzz

HONEYBEES!

Honeybees stick their tongues into coffee flowers to collect nectar, and that nectar contains low doses of caffeine.

Honeybees get caffeinated for the same reasons that we do:

 MEMORIZATION (addiction?)

Bees travel thousand of miles to collect nectar, often jumping between numerous flowers. Caffeine in the coffee flower manipulates a bee's long-term memory. A study on honeybees concluded that caffeine makes certain flowers more memorable. Because bees enjoy the stimulant, they tend to return to the caffeinated flowers more frequently.

(Honeybees are nature's little caffeine junkies.)

② PRODUCTIVITY

Since caffeinated bees remember which flowers give them the most kick, it makes them more productive and focused, because they don't waste time pollinating the wrong flowers.

③ IT'S HABIT-FORMING

Bees remember the effects of caffeine, and they develop a preference for coffee trees when collecting nectar. Sounds a bit familiar to anyone who is a slave to their coffeepot.

(Oh, honeybees, how I sympathize.)

THE POINT IS:

The next time you have a cup of coffee
and you're feeling buzzed,
remember that you're not alone.
Honeybees are right there with you.

Buzzed, get it?

Of course you do.

CHEERS!

THE TOP 10 MOST COFFEE-DRINKING COUNTRIES

ANNUAL COFFEE CONSUMPTION IN KILOGRAMS PER PERSON (2008)

Country	Consumption
FINLAND	12 KG
NORWAY	9.9 KG
ICELAND	9.0 KG
DENMARK	8.7 KG
NETHERLANDS	8.4 KG
SWEDEN	8.2 KG
SWITZERLAND	7.9 KG
BELGIUM	6.8 KG
CANADA	6.5 KG
BOSNIA AND HERZEGOVINA	6.2 KG

THE TOP 5 COFFEE-PRODUCING COUNTRIES

1 BAG WEIGHS 60 KILOGRAMS /132 POUNDS

(2010-2011 CROP YEAR)

54,500,000 BAGS

18,725,000 BAGS

9,500,000 BAGS

9,225,000 BAGS

5,100,000 BAGS

BRAZIL

VIETNAM

COLOMBIA

INDONESIA

INDIA

THE TOP 5 COFFEE-IMPORTING COUNTRIES

(2008)

 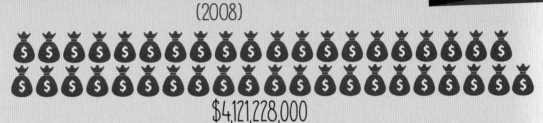

U.S.A

$4,121,228,000

GERMANY

$3,344,098,000

ITALY

$1,382,895,000

FRANCE

$1,381,309,000

JAPAN

$1,272,614,000

9 COFFEE DRINKS
WITH
CLEVER NICKNAMES
THAT YOU'VE PROBABLY NEVER HEARD OF

RED EYE

COFFEE

Coffee with a shot of
espresso poured in
(a.k.a. "Shot in the dark,"
"Depth charge")

BLACK EYE

COFFEE

Coffee with a double
espresso poured in

GREEN EYE

COFFEE

Coffee with a triple
espresso poured in
(a.k.a. "Triple death")

CAFE ZORRO

HOT WATER

1:1 ratio of hot water
to double espresso

MELANGE

WHIPPED CREAM

COFFEE

Coffee with whipped
cream on the top

DIRTY CHAI

CHAI TEA

Chai tea with a shot of
espresso poured in
(a.k.a. "Dirty hippie")

YUANYANG

MILK TEA

COFFEE

Mixture of coffee and
Hong Kong–style milk tea
(a.k.a. "Ying Yong")

EISKAFFEE

WHIPPED CREAM

VANILLA ICE CREAM

MILK & SUGAR

ICED COFFEE

German drink consisting of
iced coffee, milk,
sugar, vanilla ice cream,
and whipped cream

MIAMI VICE

HOT WATER & SUGAR

CUBANO COFFEE

AMERICANO

Mixture of Americano,
Cubano coffee,
hot water, and sugar

WHAT THAT PLATE

UNDER YOUR COFFEE
IS ACTUALLY FOR

Typically, the saucer under a coffee cup is used to carry the coffee or hold a spoon.

BUT!

In the 18th century,
coffee wasn't drunk from the cup.
They poured coffee into the saucer
to cool it off, and then slurped it
from the saucer.

Here are some old paintings that show
this crazy saucer-slurping business.

See?

William Sidney Mount (1838)

Here

Konstantin Makovsky (1914)

POINT IS

Coffee is such an awesome beverage, people used to drink it from a plate.

You should too.

COFFEE SAY ABOUT YOUR PERSONALITY?

THE BLACK COFFEE DRINKER

- STRAIGHTFORWARD
- LIKES TO KEEP THINGS SIMPLE
- QUIET, BUT MOODY
- ALL ABOUT MINIMALISM

THE ESPRESSO DRINKER

- TAKES ON LEADERSHIP
- HARDWORKING, BUT MOODY
- KNOWS HOW TO GET WHAT THEY WANT

THE LATTE DRINKER

- TENDS TO BE NEUROTIC
- LIKES TO PLEASE PEOPLE
- OFTEN INDECISIVE

THE CAPPUCCINO DRINKER

- OBSESSIVE AND CONTROLLING
- CREATIVE, HONEST, AND MOTIVATED
- MAKES EXCELLENT FRIENDS, BUT GETS BORED WITH UNIMAGINATIVE PEOPLE

THE FRAPPUCCINO DRINKER

- WILL TRY ANYTHING ONCE
- TRENDSETTER
- ADVENTUROUS AND COURAGEOUS
- DOES NOT MAKE HEALTHY CHOICES

THE INSTANT COFFEE DRINKER

- CHEERFUL AND OPTIMISTIC
- LAID-BACK
- TENDS TO PUT THINGS OFF

THE SOYMILK DRINKER

- HIGH-MAINTENANCE
- DETAIL-ORIENTED
- SELF-RIGHTEOUS AND SELF-CENTERED

Which Profession Drinks the Most Coffee?

Top 15 Heaviest Coffee Drinkers

&

Coffee Consumption Trends in the Workplace

1. Scientist/Lab Technician
2. Marketing/PR Professional
3. Education Administrator
4. Editor/Writer
5. Healthcare Administrator
6. Physician
7. Food Preparer
8. Professor
9. Social Worker
10. Financial Professional
11. Personal Caretaker
12. Human Resources Benefits Coordinator
13. Nurse
14. Government Professional
15. Skilled Tradeperson

Coffee Consumption Trends in the Workplace

46% of all U.S. workers claim they are less productive without coffee.

61% of the workers who need coffee to get through their day drink 2 cups or more each day.

49% admit to needing coffee while on the job in the Northeast, where the workday coffee ritual is the strongest.

☑ **Editors/Writers**
☑ **Government Professionals**
☑ **Teachers**

are
most likely to add flavor to their coffee.

☑ **Human Resource Professionals**
☑ **Personal Caretakers**
are
most likely to enjoy their
coffee with cream and sugar.

☑ **Judges**
☑ **Attorneys**
☑ **Hotel Workers**

are
most likely to take their
coffee black.

THE PROS AND CONS OF—

Table sugar

Pros: No chemicals, stirs easily.
Cons: Causes diabetes, which could kill you someday.

Sugar in the raw

Pros: Minimally processed and natural.
Cons: Sinks to the bottom of your cup, resulting in bitter coffee, which makes you sad, which could kill you someday.

Splenda

Pros: No aspartame.
Cons: Contains a chlorine molecule that your body may not break down, which could kill you someday.

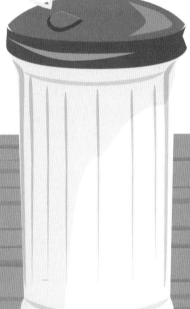

SUGAR

→FLAVORING YOUR COFFEE

Equal

Pros: Low calorie and very sweet.

Cons: Contains aspartame, which may or may not cause cancer in lab rats, and could kill you someday.

Creamer

Pros: Creamy, tasty, smooth.
Cons: High in fat, which leads to obesity, which could kill you someday.

Drinking it black

Pros: Too many to name.

Cons: Forces you to drink sharp, bitter coffee, which results in a sharp, bitter soul, which could kill you someday.

10 THINGS
YOU PROBABLY DIDN'T KNOW ABOUT
CAFFEINE

CAFFEINE IS THE MOST POPULAR AND WIDELY USED

DRUG

IN THE WORLD
(CAFFEINE IS A CRYSTALLINE WHITE POWDER IN ITS PURE STATE)

CAFFEINE KICKS IN AFTER

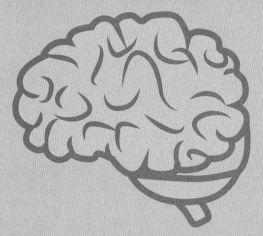

15 TO 20 MINUTES

THE EFFECTS OF CAFFEINE
CAN LAST 8 to 14 HOURS,
DEPENDING ON THE PERSON

60

DIFFERENT PLANTS
HAVE CAFFEINE IN THEM

COFFEE AND TEA ARE NOT THE ONLY ONES!

COFFEE + **15**MIN **NAP**

= BRAIN REBOOT

From *Wired's* How to Wiki:

"1. Right before you crash, down a cup of java. The caffeine has to travel through your gastro-intestinal tract, giving you time to nap before it kicks in.

2. Close your eyes and relax. Even if you only doze, you'll get what's known as effective microsleep,or momentary lapses of wakefulness.

3. Limit your nap to 15 minutes. A half hour can lead to sleep inertia, or the spinning down of the brain's prefrontal cortex, which handles functions like judgment. This gray matter can take 30 minutes to reboot."

10 TO 20 GRAMS

OF CAFFEINE IS GENERALLY CONSIDERED A LETHAL DOSE

(THE EQUIVALENT OF 4.69 GALLONS OF COFFEE)

DOES NOT MEAN ZERO CAFFEINE

Decaf still has 8.6 mg to 13.9 mg of caffeine.

A cup of regular drip coffee contains around 95 to 200 mg.

90% OF THE PEOPLE USE CAFFEINE IN SOME FORM IN THE WORLD

DIFFERENT COFFEES HAVE DIFFERENT AMOUNTS OF CAFFEINE (fl oz)

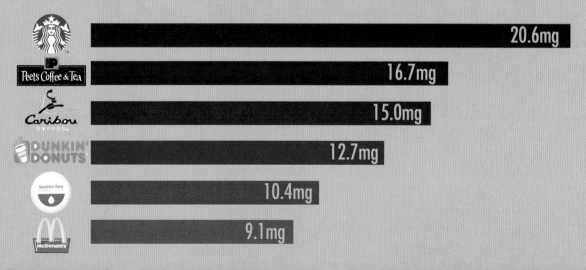

Starbucks	20.6mg
Peets Coffee & Tea	16.7mg
Caribou	15.0mg
Dunkin' Donuts	12.7mg
Seattle's Best	10.4mg
McDonald's	9.1mg

1,3,7- TRIMETHYLXANTHINE

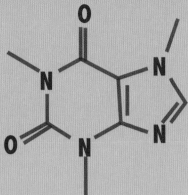

IS CAFFEINE'S CHEMICAL NAME

THERE'S MORE CAFFEINE IN COFFEE THAN MOST ENERGY DRINKS

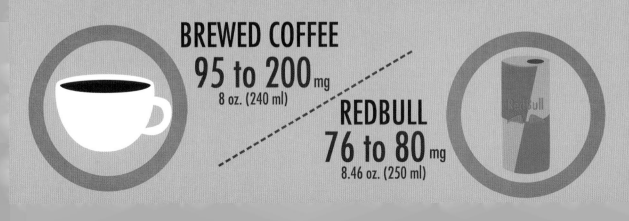

BREWED COFFEE
95 to 200 mg
8 oz. (240 ml)

REDBULL
76 to 80 mg
8.46 oz. (250 ml)

5 COMMON MISTAKES WHEN BREWING COFFEE

✕ STORING COFFEE BEANS IN THE FREEZER OR FRIDGE

PLACING COFFEE BEANS IN THE FRIDGE OR FREEZER DOESN'T HELP KEEP THEM FRESH. ROASTED BEANS HAVE COUNTLESS HOLES IN THEM AND THEY ABSORB THE MOISTURE AND THE SMELL OF OTHER FOODS IN THE FRIDGE. THE BEST WAY TO STORE BEANS IS TO KEEP THEM AT ROOM TEMPERATURE INSIDE AN AIRTIGHT CONTAINER.

✕ BUYING PRE-GROUND BEANS

PRE-GROUND BEANS ARE CONVENIENT AND EASY, BUT COFFEE BEANS START LOSING THEIR FRESHNESS IMMEDIATELY AFTER GRINDING. TO PRESERVE THE QUALITY OF THE BEANS, YOU SHOULD GRIND BEANS RIGHT BEFORE BREWING.

✕ USING BOILING WATER TO BREW COFFEE

WHEN YOU USE BOILING WATER, IT EXTRACTS BITTERNESS AND ACIDITY FROM THE BEANS. FOR BREWING, THE IDEAL TEMPERATURE IS AROUND 200°F (93°C). AN EASY TRICK TO REACH THIS TEMPERATURE IS TO BOIL WATER AND THEN WAIT 45 SECONDS.

✕ USING TOO MUCH OR TOO LITTLE COFFEE

THE PERFECT RATIO IS 2 TABLESPOONS OF COFFEE GROUNDS TO EVERY 6 oz. OF WATER.

✕ USING THE WRONG GRIND

DIFFERENT EQUIPMENT REQUIRES DIFFERENT GRINDS. FINE GRINDS ARE FOR ESPRESSO OR AEROPRESS, MEDIUM ARE FOR DRIP MAKERS, AND COARSE GRINDS ARE FOR A FRENCH PRESS.

THAT'S IT! HAPPY BREWING!

How many calories are in a drink from
STARBUCKS?

All the drinks depicted are grande sized.

Note: The following compares caloric values ONLY.
It does not compare fat, sodium, or sugar content.

PEPPERMINT
WHITE CHOCOLATE MOCHA

 = 520
CALORIES

The equivalent of 3.7 cans of COCA COLA

DOUBLE CHOCOLATY CHIP FRAPPUCCINO

 **= 500**
CALORIES

The equivalent of one hundred and twenty
SKITTLES

HOT CHOCOLATE

 = 370
CALORIES

The equivalent of forty-five
gummy bears

GREEN TEA LATTE

 = ## 350
CALORIES

The equivalent of a medium
french fry
from McDonalds

CAFE MOCHA

 = 330

CALORIES

The equivalent of one hundred and thirty
goldfish crackers

CAFE LATTE

 **= 190**

CALORIES

The equivalent of one slice of

pizza

BLACK COFFEE

 $=$ ZERO
CALORIES

The equivalent of drinking caffeinated air

Point is:

If you're counting calories, be careful what you order.

It's easy to transform your morning coffee into liquid dessert.

The various types of cappuccino

Traditional Cappuccino

foam

1/3
1/3
1/3

steamed milk

espresso

Cappuccino Chiaro

MORE STEAMED MILK AND LESS ESPRESSO

Cappuccino Scuro

MORE ESPRESSO AND LESS STEAMED MILK

Dry Cappuccino

MORE FOAM AND LESS STEAMED MILK

Wet Cappuccino

MORE STEAMED MILK AND LESS FOAM

Amount of Foam

LOTS OF FOAM

Dry

Cappuccino

Chiaro

Scuro

Wet

Latte

LESS FOAM

10 COFFEE MYTHS and FACTS

COFFEE MAKES YOU POOP

☕ TRUE! ☕

Coffee is a powerful stimulant that can help prevent constipation and keep bowel movements regular.

The effect is the same for both caffeinated and decaffeinated brews.

Coffee can also cause loose bowel movements, however, so be careful!

KEEPING COFFEE GRINDS OR BEANS IN THE FREEZER IS A GOOD IDEA

☕ FALSE! ☕

Keeping beans in the freezer results in condensation, which in turn results in loss of flavor. It is, however, advisable to keep your beans out of the heat if you live in a warm climate. The best way to store them is to keep them at room temperature inside an airtight container.

COFFEE FIXES HANGOVERS

♥ FALSE! ♥

Caffeine will help to wake up a sleepy drunk, but it won't help them feel any better the morning after. In fact, since a hangover is caused by severe dehydration from alcohol, coffee can actually make a hangover worse by dehydrating the body further.

COFFEE CAN HELP RETAIN MEMORY

♥ TRUE! ♥

In a study where caffeine equal to 2 cups of coffee was given to participants, MRI scans showed that "brain activity was increased in two locations—the memory-rich frontal lobe and the attention-controlling anterior cingulum." Coffee can temporarily enhance your focus and memory, which is good to know for the next time you need to concentrate or take a test.

COFFEE IS LIKELY TO CAUSE INSOMNIA

☕ FALSE! ☕

Coffee can keep you alert for a few hours, but if you're drinking it before midday, it's probably not the cause of your insomnia. Your body quickly absorbs caffeine, but it gets rid of it quickly, too. After 8 to 10 hours, 75% of the caffeine is gone from your body and you should be able to fall asleep without any trouble.

DRINKING COFFEE IS AN AID TO WEIGHT LOSS

☕ TRUE! ☕

Caffeine can boost the metabolic rate and the rate of fat breakdown in the short term. Caffeine causes muscles to use fat as fuel, which may be the reason why your body burns extra calories when you drink coffee.

COFFEE MAKES WOMEN'S BREASTS SMALLER

☕ TRUE! ☕

According to Swedish oncologist Dr. Helena Jernstroem, drinking more than
3 cups of coffee a day can reduce the size of a woman's breasts.
Those with unwanted man boobs or seeking breast reduction, take note.

COFFEE IS NOT GOOD FOR
PREGNANT WOMEN

☕ TRUE! ☕

Women who are expecting a baby should not drink more than one 12-oz.
cup of coffee a day. Too much caffeine can reduce blood flow to the placenta,
reducing the amount of oxygen and nutrients a baby receives.
It may also cause an irregular heartbeat in the fetus.
Best to stick to decaffeinated brews during this time.

COFFEE HELPS REDUCE STRESS

♥ FALSE! ♥

Though you may crave a good coffee during stressful times,
it could be a bad idea. For those prone to panic attacks and anxiety
in particular, caffeine will increase and enhance the effects of stress.

CAFFEINE IS ADDICTIVE

♥ FALSE! ♥

According to the WHO, "There is no evidence whatsoever that caffeine use has
even remotely comparable physical and social consequences which are
associated with serious drugs of abuse." HOWEVER, I also found many articles
and studies saying caffeine is addictive because it causes dependence.
Therefore, if you decide to quit drinking coffee you should do so gradually
to avoid headaches, anxiety, and irritability.

So, I say it's also  ♥ **TRUE!** ♥

WHY IS COFFEE CALLED

A CUP OF JOE ?

WAS JOE THE FIRST MAN TO TEAR DOWN A COFFEE TREE
AND BREW THAT BAD BOY INTO A TASTY BEVERAGE? → NOPE!

WAS THERE A POPULAR BRAND CALLED "JOE'S COFFEE"
AT SOME POINT IN TIME? → STILL NOPE!

DID "A CUP OF JIM" SOUND WEIRD?

→ WELL, YES, BUT THAT'S STILL NOT WHY.

THIS IS JOE.

HIS FULL NAME WAS

JOSEPHUS DANIELS.

AND IN ADDITION TO BEING WICKED HANDSOME,
HE WAS THE 41ST SECRETARY
OF THE UNITED STATES NAVY.

DANIELS WAS A VERY STRICT AND RIGHTEOUS MAN
WHO WANTED TO BRING MORALS TO THE NAVY LIFE.
HE BANNED BOOZE ON ALL SHIPS ON JUNE 1, 1914.

(HE ALSO BANNED CONDOMS TO KEEP HIS SAILORS AWAY FROM THE LADIES.)

 = LOVE SAUCE FROM THE **DEVIL**

SO, COFFEE BECAME A CLEAN AND RIGHTEOUS
SUBSTITUTE FOR BOOZE AND DEBAUCHERY.

 = BEAN JUICE FROM JESUS

LEGEND HAS IT,
SAILORS SOON STARTED SARCASTICALLY
REFERRING TO COFFEE AS
"A CUP OF JOSEPHUS DANIELS."

THIS EVENTUALLY GOT
SHORTENED TO

"A CUP OF JOE,"

AND THE NAME STUCK.

(CONDOMS REMAINED CONDOMS, THOUGH,
RATHER THAN BECOMING A "SOCK OF JOE.")

IF COFFEE WERE MY
BOYFRIEND

WRITTEN BY RYOKO IWATA, DRAWN BY THE OATMEAL

EVERY MORNING HE'D WAKE ME UP TO A FANTASTIC AROMA . . .

INSTEAD OF A FOUL ONE.

83

WE'D BE BEST BUDDIES, ESPECIALLY AT WORK.

AND HE'D MAKE ME **WAY** MORE RECEPTIVE TO OTHER PEOPLE'S IDEAS.

WE SHOULD BUILD AN APP THAT TALLIES UP THE NUMBER OF SMILES YOU SEE EACH DAY, AND THEN EACH WEEK YOU'D HAVE A SMILEY SCORE!

KEEP SPEAKING AND I WILL TURN YOUR VERTEBRAE INTO A LAWN ORNAMENT.

SORRY ABOUT THAT. CAN YOU GIVE US 5 MINUTES?

EVENTUALLY I'D COME TO RELY ON HIM FOR ANY SORT OF PRODUCTIVITY...

HEY, WANNA GO GRAB SOME COFFEE FROM THAT PLACE ACROSS THE STREET?

HOLD UP. I REQUIRE COFFEE BEFORE I CAN GO GET MY COFFEE.

AS WELL AS SOME OTHER THINGS.

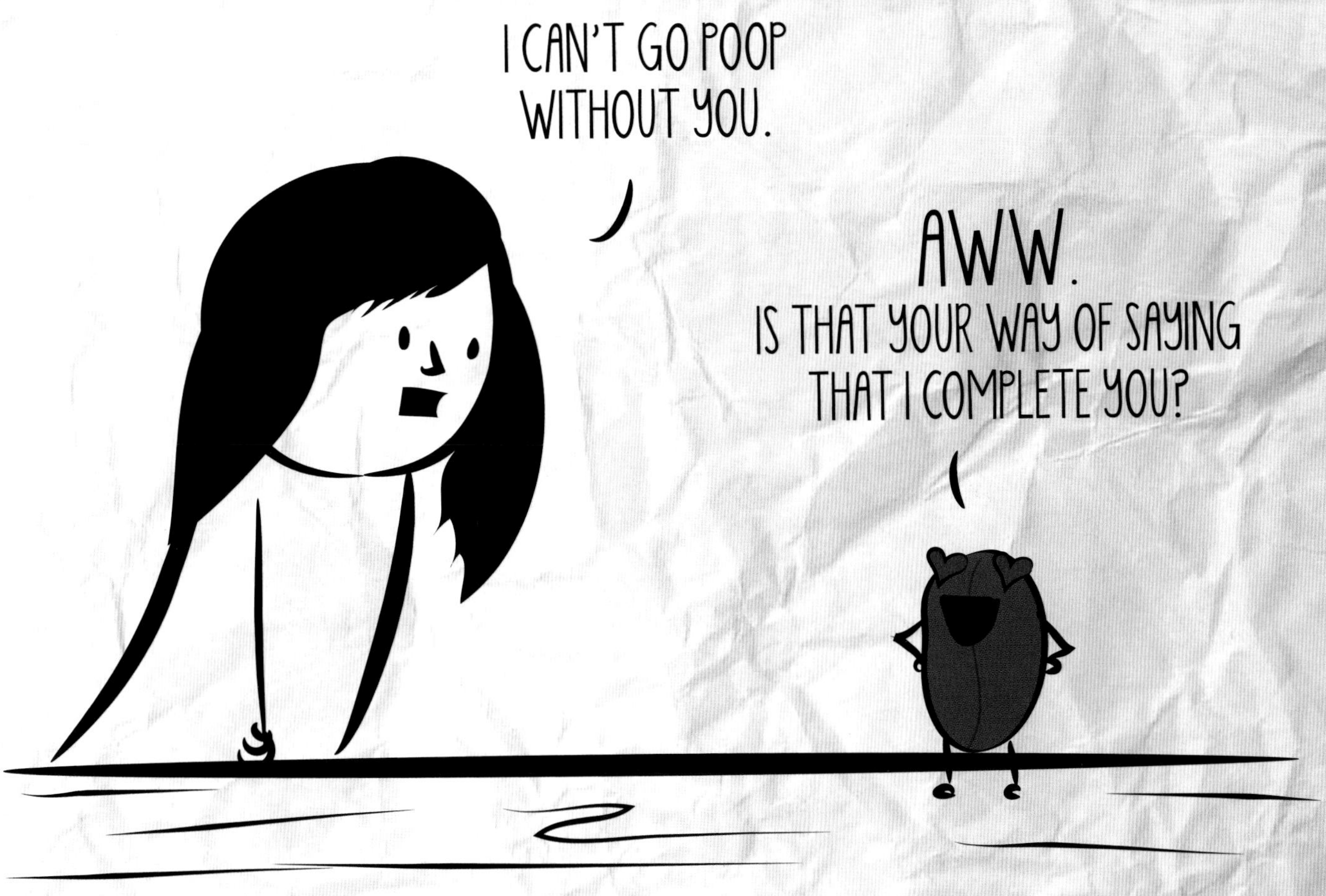

IF COFFEE WERE MY BOYFRIEND, HE'D GIVE ME SUPERPOWERS.

FLY UPWARD!

CLEAN SURFACES!

TYPE WORDS!

TAP TAP
TAP

BUILD STRUCTURES!

TRY TO SLEEP!

DANCE PARTY
INSTEAD!

BOUNCE
BOUNCE
BOUNCE

89

THESE SUPERPOWERS COULD BE USED FOR

GOOD,

EVIL,

REFERENCES

YOUR BRAIN ON BEER VS. COFFEE
Mikael Cho, *Coffee vs. Beer: Which Drink Makes You More Creative?*, medium.com/what-i-learned-today/coffee-vs-beer-which-drink-makes-you-more-creative-f7fcb3b786b1

THE BEST TIME TO DRINK COFFEE ACCORDING TO SCIENCE
Steven Miller Ph.D., *The Best Time for Your Coffee*, neurosciencedc.blogspot.com/2013/10/the-best-time-for-your-coffee.html

Gizmodo, *The Scientifically Best Time to Drink Coffee*, gizmodo.com/the-scientifically-best-time-to-drink-coffee-1460030914

New York Daily News, *Best Time to Drink Coffee Isn't First Thing in the Morning*, www.nydailynews.com/life-style/health/scientist-unveils-best-time-drink-coffee-article-1.1509821

20 NEATO FACTS WORTH KNOWING ABOUT COFFEE
Discover Magazine, *20 Things You Didn't Know about Coffee*, discovermagazine.com/2013/april/22-20-things-you-didnt-know-about-coffee#.

Kitchen Daily, *15 Things You Didn't Know about Coffee*, www.kitchendaily.com/read/history-facts-and-health-benefits-coffee-beans

Government Executive, *11 Things You Didn't Know about Drinking Coffee at Work*, www.govexec.com/excellence/promising-practices/2013/04/11-things-you-didnt-know-about-drinking-coffee-work/62366/

Coffee News, *Coffee Trivia*, coffeenewsdallas.com/get-involved/coffee-trivia/

Coffee Lovers United, *17 Fun Facts about Coffee: Some Weird, Interesting, Untold Coffee-Facts*, coffeeloversunited.com/17-fun-facts-about-coffee-some-weird-interesting-untold-coffee-facts/

Skinny Coffee Works, *Fan Facts & Trivia about Coffee*, www.skinnycoffeeworks.com/coffee-facts-trivia.html

A MAP OF WHICH U.S. STATES HAVE THE MOST STARBUCKS
StateMaster, *Starbucks Stores (per capita)*, www.statemaster.com/graph/lif_sta_sto_percap-lifestyle-starbucks-stores-per-capita

ESPRESSO DRINKS 101
Wikipedia, *Espresso*, en.wikipedia.org/wiki/Espresso

HONEYBEES ARE NATURE'S LITTLE COFFEE ADDICTS
Christy Ullrich, *National Geographic, Bees Buzzing on Caffeine*, news.nationalgeographic.com/news/2013/03/130308-bees-caffeine-animal-behavior-science

THE TOP 10 MOST COFFEE-DRINKING COUNTRIES
Maps of World, *Top Coffee Importing Countries in the World*, www.mapsofworld.com/world-maps/top-coffee-importing-countries.html

Bloomberg, *World's Top 10 Coffee-Producing Countries in 2010-2011*, www.bloomberg.com/news/2011-08-19/world-s-top-10-coffee-producing-countries-in-2010-2011-table-.html

WorldMapper.org, *Coffee Consumption*, www.worldmapper.org/posters/worldmapper_1038_coffee_consumption_ver2.pdf

9 COFFEE DRINKS WITH CLEVER NICKNAMES THAT YOU'VE PROBABLY NEVER HEARD OF
Wikipedia, *List of Coffee Beverages*, en.wikipedia.org/wiki/List_of_coffee_beverages

WHAT THAT PLATE UNDER YOUR COFFEE IS ACTUALLY FOR
Wikipedia, *Saucer*, ja.wikipedia.org/wiki/soucer

RocketNews24, rocketnews24.com/2012/05/08/210302

WHAT DOES YOUR FAVORITE COFFEE SAY ABOUT YOUR PERSONALITY?
Daily Mail, *What Does Your Coffee Say about You?*, www.dailymail.co.uk/news/article-2426126/What-does-coffee-say-Cappuccino-lovers-likely-obsessive--latte-drinkers-try-others.html

Sydney Morning Herald, Coffee: your personality in a cup, www.smh.com.au/news/entertainment/good-living/can-coffee-predict-personality/2010/02/08/1265477586158.html

Aquaterra, *What Your Cup of Coffee Says about You*, www.aquaterracorp.ca/page.aspx?name=CupOfCoffeeE

WHICH PROFESSIONS DRINK THE MOST COFFEE?

Dunkin' Donuts, *New Dunkin' Donuts and CareerBuilder Survey Reveals Which Professionals Need Coffee the Most,* www.dunkindonuts.com/DDBlog/2011/09/new_dunkin_donuts.html#sthash.h5uKD1po.dpbs

THE PROS AND CONS OF FLAVORING YOUR COFFEE

Michael R. Eades, M.D., *Splenda Misinformation,* http://www.proteinpower.com/drmike/sugar-and-sweeteners/splenda-misinformation/

Dr. Janet Starr Hull, *The Hidden Chemicals in Splenda,* http://www.janethull.com/newsletter/1205/the_hidden_chemicals_in_splenda.php

Medical News Today, *Aspartame Causes Cancer in Rats at Levels Currently Approved for Humans,* http://www.medicalnewstoday.com/releases/34040

National Cancer Institute, *Artificial Sweeteners and Cancer,* http://www.cancer.gov/cancertopics/factsheet/Risk/artificial-sweeteners

ScienceDaily, *Artificial sweetener causes cancer in rats at levels currently approved for humans, new study suggests,* http://www.sciencedaily.com/releases/2006/02/060213093019.htm

10 THINGS YOU PROBABLY DIDN'T KNOW ABOUT CAFFEINE

Lifehacker, *Reboot Your Brain with a Caffeine Nap,* lifehacker.com/306029/reboot-your-brain-with-a-caffeine-nap

Huffington Post, *How Much Caffeine Is Actually in Your Coffee, from Dunkin' to Starbucks,* www.huffingtonpost.com/thrillist/caffeine-in-coffee_b_3671665.html

About.com, *Fast Facts about Caffeine,* coffeetea.about.com/cs/caffeine/a/caffeinefacts.htm

National Geographic Magazine http://ngm.nationalgeographic.com/ngm/0501/feature1/

5 COMMON MISTAKES WHEN BREWING COFFEE

Huffington Post, *To Freeze Coffee or Not? 7 Myths about Making Coffee Answered,* www.huffingtonpost.com/eatingwell/7-coffee-myths_b_911913.html

Huffington Post, *How to Make Coffee: Mistakes Not to Make,* www.huffingtonpost.com/2013/04/17/how-to-coffee-mistakes_n_3093745.html

HOW MANY CALORIES ARE IN A DRINK FROM STARBUCKS?

Starbucks, *Nutrition,* www.starbucks.com/menu/nutrition, February 2014

10 COFFEE MYTHS AND FACTS

Moss Greene, BellaOnline, *20 Coffee and Caffeine Myths and Facts,* www.bellaonline.com/articles/art31354.asp

WebMD, *Caffeine Myths and Facts,* www.webmd.com/balance/caffeine-myths-and-facts?page=2

Live Strong http://www.livestrong.com/article/460409-does-caffeine-increase-your-metabolism/

Authority Nutrition http://authoritynutrition.com/coffee-increase-metabolism/

WHY IS COFFEE CALLED A CUP OF JOE?

TheKitchn, *The Man Named Josephus: Why We Call Coffee "A Cup of Joe,"* www.thekitchn.com/the-man-named-josephus-why-we-call-coffee-a-cup-of-joe-190244

Zachary M. Seward, Quartz, *Why Coffee Is Called "Joe,"* qz.com/88453/why-coffee-is-called-joe/

SPECIAL THANKS TO MATTHEW INMAN, THE OATMEAL, FOR HELPING ME WITH THIS BOOK AND FOR DRAWING THE CUTEST COFFEE COMIC, *IF COFFEE WERE MY BOYFRIEND.* THIS BOOK AND *I LOVE COFFEE* EXIST BECAUSE OF YOU, ARIGATO! ALSO THANKS TO PATTY RICE, MY LOVELY EDITOR, WHO GUIDED ME THROUGH THE ENTIRE PROCESS WITH INCREDIBLE PATIENCE AND EXPERTISE. LASTLY, HUGS TO MY FELLOW COFFEE LOVERS FROM ALL OVER THE WORLD.

LOVE,
RYOKO

COFFEE GIVES ME SUPERPOWERS

Andrews McMeel Publishing, LLC
an Andrews McMeel Universal company
1130 Walnut Street, Kansas City, Missouri 64106

www.andrewsmcmeel.com

15 16 17 18 19 QGR 10 9 8 7 6 5 4 3 2

ISBN: 978-1-4494-6083-9

Library of Congress Control Number: 2014946031

This book contains references to registered and unregistered third-party trademarks and service marks. All of the third-party trademarks and service marks contained in this book are the property of their respective owners. This book is not in any way endorsed by, or affiliated with, any such third-party owners.

ATTENTION: SCHOOLS AND BUSINESSES
Andrews McMeel books are available at quantity discounts with bulk purchase for educational, business, or sales promotional use. For information, please e-mail the Andrews McMeel Publishing Special Sales Department: specialsales@amuniversal.com.